W9-CKI-363

Mar'22   6/0/0

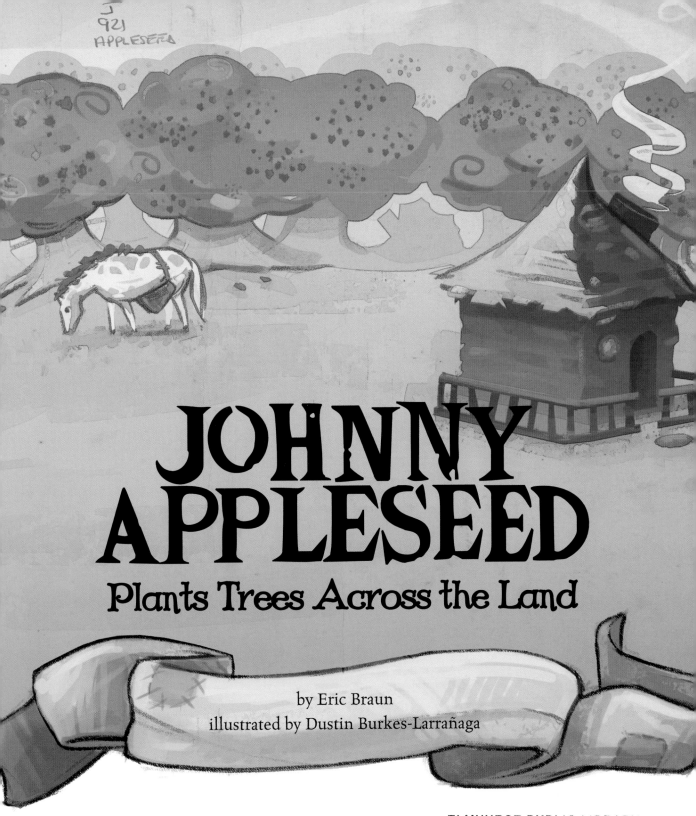

# JOHNNY APPLESEED

## Plants Trees Across the Land

by Eric Braun

illustrated by Dustin Burkes-Larrañaga

PICTURE WINDOW BOOKS

a capstone imprint

# JOHN CHAPMAN

## Wandering Planter

When the United States of America was young, much of its land was wild frontier. Pioneers set out to claim land for their families. One of the pioneers was a man named John Chapman. John was born in Massachusetts in the late 1700s. He spent most of his life wandering in the wilderness of Pennsylvania, Ohio, and Indiana. But he wasn't just wandering. Everywhere he went, he planted apple trees.

The apple trees John planted provided food for people. Just like John spread apples throughout the land, people spread stories about him. They said he was kind, peaceful, strong, and humble. They called him "Johnny Appleseed."

After John died in 1845, his stories grew. Johnny Appleseed soon became an American legend.

If you saw John Chapman as a young'un in Massachusetts, you'd never guess he'd grow up to be a pioneer. Right skinny feller he was. Didn't know much about travelin' or explorin'. Yessiree, John was as happy as a worm in an apple right there in his dad's apple orchard.

One day John learned about the pioneers headin' west
to settle new land. They needed apples for food and tradin'.

Soon John had a dream, and he told his brother all about it. "Beautiful apple orchards will rise all over the frontier!" he said, grinnin' with joy. "And I will be the one to plant them."

John gathered up as many apple seeds as he could. He pulled them from the cider press. Then he asked neighbors for their seeds. Them seeds was like trash to folks.

Eventually, he had collected enough seeds. He put them
in a leather bag, and then he headed west.

Now, if you saw John Chapman headin' into the wild all alone, you still wouldn't think he looked like much of a pioneer. Shoot, most folks said he was downright funny lookin'. His long, dark beard was a tangled mess. He wore a tin pot for a hat and an old coffee sack for a shirt. He didn't even wear shoes.

Don't you mind what he looked like though. He was seein' his dream come true. He headed toward the Ohio River Valley—deep into the frontier.

John Chapman found a perfect spot along the splashin' shores of Lickin' Creek to start his work. He was the only person 'round for miles and miles. The trees made a thick web overhead. Clouds of bugs buzzed in the air as he inched his shovel into the soil.

John dropped seeds, covered them with dirt, and watered them. Then he moseyed on down the creek to plant more.

For years John walked all over the frontier, plantin' apple seeds. He got to be a right welcome sight for families livin' there. If you think that's because John brought good things with him, you're darn tootin'.

John sold seeds and trees to those who needed them. If people didn't have enough money, well, he just gave them what they needed anyway.

John didn't bring only apples and trees and seeds. He brought stories and goodwill too.

The children always asked, "What did you bring us today, Johnny Appleseed?" That's what people had started callin' him.

Johnny Appleseed gave ribbons and other gifts to the children. He stuck pins in his feet to entertain them. "My feet are so tough from walkin', nothin' can hurt them!" he said.

"Johnny," the adults said, "would you stay in our home tonight? We have a warm fire and a warm meal for you."

Johnny Appleseed was so kind and wise, people wanted to help him. But most of the time, he preferred to eat and sleep alone outside—even in winter.

"No, thank you," he said. "The starry sky will be my shelter tonight. I'll cook my meal in my own pot."

American Indians welcomed Johnny Appleseed to their villages. Though natives and pioneers often distrusted each other, they trusted Johnny. He brought them gifts, stories, and good cheer—same as he did everywhere he went.

"You can plant an orchard with these seeds," Johnny said.

After a visit he'd be on his way, wanderin' barefoot through the countryside. That was just the way he liked it.

One day he was wanderin' through a field, just a-hummin' a
tune to himself. Right then he saw a farmer about to shoot his
own horse!

"What's the trouble?" Johnny asked.

"It's old Bernadette, here," the farmer replied. "Her leg's broken."
Johnny Appleseed knew just what to do. He healed Bernadette's
leg and helped her get strong again. People said Johnny could heal
anythin' using nothin' but his hands.

Not long after he helped that horse, Johnny heard a wolf wailin'
in pain. Now if you ever heard that sound, you know it ain't pretty.
"Ah-ooooooooo-ch!"

That sound made Johnny plumb sad, so he went into the woods
to find that wailin' wolf. When he tracked it down, he saw that it
was caught in a hunter's trap. You can bet your apple dumplin's he
freed that wolf, fed it, and healed its leg! The wolf was so grateful,
it followed Johnny everywhere he went.

Johnny kept on wanderin' and plantin' seeds—but now he had a wolf as a pet!

Remember when Johnny planted the first seeds along Lickin' Creek? Well, after almost 40 years of plantin', the area was a-changin'. A whole mess of families had settled in the woods. Towns and churches had popped up. Roads split the forest, and stagecoaches carried more folks into the area. The coaches also carried food.

Not only that, but Johnny's apple trees were growin' all over the land. He decided it was time to make the long walk to Indiana. That was the frontier now. That was where he and his apple seeds were needed.

In the summer of 1847, Johnny spent the night with a kindly family in Indiana. He told them stories before bed. He must've been plumb tuckered out, because he stayed with them in their warm house that night.

In the mornin', when the family awoke, Johnny was still lyin' by the fire. His limbs were as strong as tree branches. His skin was as shiny as an apple.

Johnny Appleseed had grown very old, and his time here on Earth was up. It was a right sad day, but not too sad. After all, Johnny Appleseed had followed his dream. When you see an apple orchard or bite into a shiny Red Delicious, you can close your eyes and thank him.

John Chapman was born on September 26, 1774, in Leominster, Massachusetts. When he was about 15 years old, he moved with his family to western Pennsylvania. A few years later, he began planting apple seeds on the frontier.

Within a few years, he was famous among the pioneers. His seeds, trees, and apples helped them survive. John had become very wealthy from selling these things. He owned much land and kept his money in jars instead of a bank. But he continued to live simply.

All across the frontier, stories about Johnny Appleseed spread by word of mouth. By the time he died in 1847, many of those stories told of him as a magical, larger-than-life man.

The first published story about Johnny Appleseed appeared in *Harper's New Monthly Magazine* in 1871. The author, W.D. Haley, told the famous stories about Johnny. In 1928 the poet Vachel Lindsay published a poem, "Johnny Appleseed," that celebrated Johnny's life.

Since then Johnny Appleseed has inspired many stories, poems, plays, and movies. They all describe John as generous, strong, and brave. And that's why Americans still remember him today. Johnny Appleseed is a symbol of American courage and kindness.

# Learn More About Folktales

Although there are many different American folktales, each story contains similar pieces. Take a look at what usually makes up an American folktale:

**hero**—the main character of an American folktale is most often a hero with exaggerated abilities, or abilities that seem greater than they actually are

**humor**—most early American folktales are funny; the exaggerated characters and situations add to the humor

**hyperbole**—exaggeration; used in folktales to make the characters seem larger than life, almost magical

**quest**—a challenge; most early American folktales include a challenge that the main character faces; the challenge may include defeating a villain

**slang**—words and phrases that are more often used in speech, and are usually used by a certain group of people; common cowboy slang consisted of words and sayings such as "There's no use beatin' the devil around the stump," which meant there's no use avoiding a difficult task

# Critical Thinking Using the Common Core

1. American folktales often include a character going on a quest. What is Johnny's quest in this story? (Key Ideas and Details)

2. If you could retell a story from your past, what details would you include and why? Which common folktale elements could you use to make the story even more exciting? (Integration of Knowledge and Ideas)

# Glossary

**darn tootin'**—absolutely right

**folktale**—a traditional, timeless tale people enjoy telling

**frontier**—the far edge of a settled area, where few people live

**goodwill**—friendly, cooperative attitude

**humble**—not proud

**legend**—a story handed down from earlier times; legends may be based on facts, but they are not entirely true

**pioneer**—a person who explores unknown territory and makes a home there

**plumb**—completely

**publish**—to create a book or other printed form of communication and make it available to the public

# Read More

**Blair, Eric, retold by**. *Johnny Appleseed*. My First Classic Story. Mankato, Minn.: Picture Window Books, 2011.

**Powell, Martin, retold by**. *The Legend of Johnny Appleseed: The Graphic Novel*. Graphic Spin. Minneapolis: Stone Arch Books, 2010.

**Shepherd, Jodie**. *Johnny Appleseed*. New York: Scholastic, 2010.

Thanks to our advisers for their expertise, research, and advice:

Elizabeth Tucker Gould, Professor of English
Binghamton University

Terry Flaherty, PhD, Professor of English
Minnesota State University, Mankato

Editor: Shelly Lyons
Designer: Tracy Davies McCabe
Art Director: Nathan Gassman
Production Specialist: Jennifer Walker
The illustrations in this book were created with pen and ink with watercolor wash.

Design element: Shutterstock: 06photo

Picture Window Books are published by Capstone,
1710 Roe Crest Drive, North Mankato, Minnesota 56003
www.capstonepub.com

Library of Congress Cataloging-in-Publication Data
Braun, Eric, 1971- author.
Johnny Appleseed plants trees across the land /
by Eric Braun.
pages cm. — (Picture window books. American folk legends)
Summary: Relates the life of John Chapman, known as Johnny Appleseed, who is famed for his distribution of apple seeds and trees across America.
ISBN 978-1-4795-5428-7 (library binding)
ISBN 978-1-4795-5445-4 (paperback)
ISBN 978-1-4795-5453-9 (eBook PDF)
1. Appleseed, Johnny, 1774-1845—Juvenile literature.
2. Apple growers—United States—Biography—Juvenile literature. 3. Frontier and pioneer life—Middle West—Juvenile literature. I. Title.
SB63.C46B64 2015
634'.11'092—dc23                    2013050827

Printed in the United States of America
in North Mankato, MN.
032014      008087CGF14

# Internet Sites

FactHound offers a safe, fun way to find Internet sites related to this book. All of the sites on FactHound have been researched by our staff.

Here's all you do:

Visit *www.facthound.com*

Type in this code: 9781479554287

Check out projects, games and lots more at
www.capstonekids.com

# Look for all the books in the series:

**Davy Crockett and the Great Mississippi Snag**
**John Henry vs. the Mighty Steam Drill**
**Johnny Appleseed Plants Trees Across the Land**
**Pecos Bill Tames a Colossal Cyclone**